BELOVED YOUNG PEOPLE

POPE JOHN PAUL II
speaks to the world's youth

BELOVED YOUNG PEOPLE

POPE JOHN PAUL II
speaks to
the world's youth

The words of
POPE JOHN PAUL II

Photographs by
VITTORIANO RASTELLI

Designed by
VANNA BRISTOT

HODDER AND STOUGHTON
LONDON SYDNEY AUCKLAND TORONTO

Contents

All excerpts taken from speeches and dialogues in General Audiences or from particular meetings with youth either in Rome or while on his journeys around the world.

To Schoolchildren and Students

Your age represents a season of preparation and apprenticeship in order to cope successfully with future responsibilities which life will hold in store for you.

⊹

I have been told that the young desire words of certainty in the difficult path of life — well, my deep desire is precisely to strengthen your faith and your hope.

⊹

I am close to each and every one of you with great affection, so that you may be able to travel the one true way and choose the one certainty which is Jesus Christ, man's Redeemer.

⊹

Man, in fact, can do without many things, but he cannot renounce those certainties which alone give his existence value. Certainty springs from the Truth and the Truth is such that it leads to Life. Jesus Christ is precisely the Way that leads to the Truth and he is 'true' because he is Life and gives Life. All men are called to pass along this Way, we are all pupils of this Master, who has words of Eternal Life.

⊹

Therefore I would like to recommend one thing to you: live these years with commitment and with joy, so that they will not be empty but rich in content; live them in study and in prayer and in the deepening of your Christian faith.

⊹

Only in this way can they constitute a valuable and fruitful reserve for future years. For complete maturity of person, you must endeavour now and always to grow inwardly, to practise virtues, to be generous and not selfish, to love others and learn to serve them, to contribute to social peace and in general to a better world. Then your joy will be great.

Isaiah 58. 6–10:
Is not this the sort of fast that pleases me
– it is the Lord Yahweh who speaks–
to break unjust fetters
and undo the thongs of the yoke,

To let the oppressed go free,
and break every yoke,
to share your bread with the hungry,
and shelter the homeless poor,

To clothe the man you see to be naked
and not turn from your own kin?
then will your light shine like the dawn
and your wound be quickly healed over.

Your integrity will go before you
and the glory of Yahweh behind you,
Cry, and Yahweh will answer;
call, and he will say, 'I am here'.

✠

May these words, boys and girls and young people, be your luminous programme. And may the Lord help you to carry it out every day while I willingly impart to you my fatherly Blessing.

I exhort the world of intellectuals, students in universities and schools and young people in general, to consider their lives not only in terms of a thorough personal formation, but as a real vocation as promoters of human and moral elevation in society, to make it more worthy, more just, more adapted to the complete man.

⊹

Apply yourselves to study with great industry. Remember that, even among adults, the man who is always prepared to learn is great, while the one who already thinks he knows everything is, actually, only full of himself and therefore empty of the great values that really enrich life.

⊹

Always establish and maintain a relationship of great and true affection with your parents; they are your first friends.

⊹

Always rest assured that the Pope loves you! I greet you all together with your teachers and parents. May the Lord always accompany you with his grace which I ask for you in abundance while I willingly grant my special Apostolic Blessing to you all.

I know that students all over the world are troubled by the problems that weigh on society around them and on the whole world. Look at those problems, explore them, study them and accept them as a challenge. But do it in the light of Christ. He put all human life in the true dimension of truth and of authentic love. True knowledge and true freedom are in Jesus.

✠

Enjoy the privileges of your youth; the right to be dynamic, creative and spontaneous; the right to be full of hope and joy; the opportunity to explore the marvellous world of science and knowledge; and above all the chance to give of yourself to others in generous and joyful service. God bless you and may the joy of Jesus be always with you!

You know that Jesus withdrew to the wilderness in prayer for forty days. Well, beloved young people, you too try to create a little silence in your lives, in order to be able to think, reflect and pray. It is difficult because we are caught up in the hubbub of events, the communications media, in such a way that inner peace is compromised and supreme thoughts are hampered. It is difficult, but it is possible and important to be able to do so.

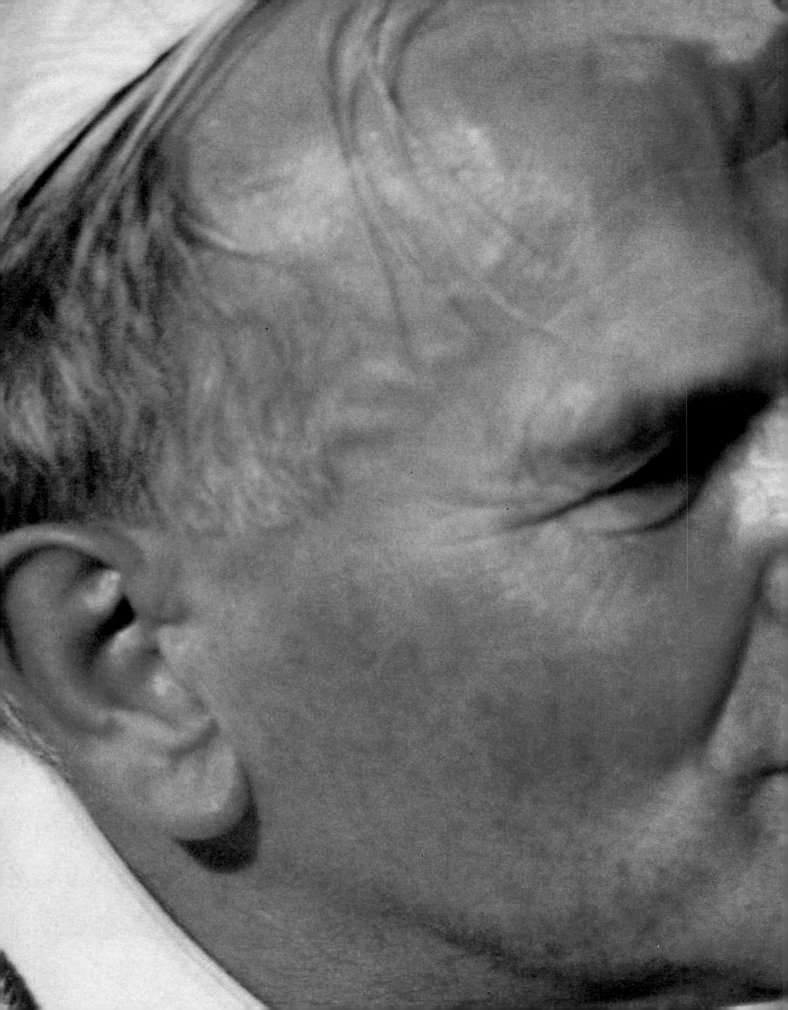

I am happy to meet you as I like to meet young Christians to witness their human and religious vitality and encourage their faith. Jesus said to Peter, 'Strengthen your brothers'. This is what I wish to do to you. I give you two simple instructions. On the one hand, take root in faith, in the faith of the Church. It is a question for you of accepting the message of Christ, which cannot be invented, of grafting your life onto his, of entering with him into a personal relationship with the Father, with your brothers, of reproducing his way of loving. We cannot learn that from the world that doubts or does not believe, or lets itself be guided solely by its impressions and immediate pleasure. Moments of reflection, of prayer, are necessary among Christians, with the chaplain, at school and in the parish, round the word of God and the sacraments. The rich sap that comes to us from Jesus, through the Apostles Peter and Paul, through saints like Francis and Clare, must be found again. That is what you must always do. In this way you will strengthen your identity as a Christian which would otherwise be shaken or impoverished. On the other hand, you will become thereby witnesses to Christ. For the world needs to know the Good News through you: through the witness of your faith in Jesus Christ – through your pure and joyful life, completely available to welcome your brothers to whom you are really able to give your attention, your time and your help. Christ calls you to follow him – I echo his call. May Christ be your joy and your strength! I bless you from the bottom of my heart, together with your educators in the faith!

Dear young people: be bearers of the 'message of Truth' in the world, be witnesses to Christ, the Way, the Truth, and the Life, the Light of the world and the salvation of mankind! By your example, show everyone that the truth must be loved! The truth must be known and therefore sought with love, dedication and method, and above all the truth must be lived. Christianity is not just a doctrine: it is first of all a Person, Jesus Christ, who must be loved and consequently imitated and realised in everyday life by means of complete faith in his word, the life of grace, prayer and charity.

Beloved young people: continue to live in the Truth and for the Truth! May the Blessed Virgin, the Seat of Wisdom, Mother of the Word who enlightens every man, assist you, enlighten you and comfort you. With these wishes, I impart to you my Apostolic Blessing.

Beloved young people: to you I wish to entrust today a commitment and a charge: be now and always transmitters of Christian joy! Above all, bear Christian joy in your hearts; joy that springs from faith serenely accepted; intensely explored by means of personal meditation and study of the Word of God and the teaching of the Church; dynamically lived in union with God in Christ, in prayer and in constant practice of the sacraments, especially the Eucharist and Reconciliation; in assimilation of the Gospel message, which is sometimes difficult for our weak human nature, which is not always in harmony with the requirements, exalting indeed but exacting, of the Sermon on the Mount and the Beatitudes. St. Augustine tells us 'Do not rejoice in earthly reality, rejoice in Christ, rejoice in his word, rejoice in his law . . . There will be peace and tranquillity in the Christian heart; but only as long as our faith is watchful; if, however, our faith sleeps, we are in danger.' The dangers, that the faith of Christians may have phases of sluggishness, are always present, especially in these periods of deep and far-reaching changes in the cultural, social, political and economic fields. But you, beloved young people, are certainly not afraid, far less ashamed, to be, and to show that you are, Christians, always and everywhere!

✠

Bring Christian joy to the environment in which you live normally, that is to your families, your associations, but especially to the scholastic world.

✠

With what hope, what respect, but also what anxiety, the citizens of a well ordered State look to the school, the place in which the young, gathered together, can seek the truth together and make of all the knowledge

acquired a unified synthesis, which will give them the capacity of judging and interpreting various and complex social and cultural situations.

Unfortunately – it is a complaint that we hear repeated very often – the modern school is going through a crisis and, sometimes, it gives mistaken information and a bad education; while the modern media of social communication, on their part, disseminate from their 'chairs' their 'lessons' of hedonism, indifferentism and materialism and try to win over and convert the young particularly.

May your presence in the world of the school, and in the wider one of culture, inspire real interests in the sphere of the various branches of knowledge, in respect for pluralism, but in the firm conviction that culture must aim at the complete perfection of the human being and the real good of the community and of the whole of human society.

Live in close communion with the men of your time; try to comprehend their way of thinking and feeling; succeed in harmonizing the knowledge of science, culture and the most recent discoveries with morality and Christian thought. Commit yourselves, young people, with your study, your preparation, your earnestness, your enthusiasm and your example, to sustaining the faith of your fellow students. This will be a highly meritorious work before God and the Church. On these foundations, construct, day by day, your present, which prepares and is a prelude to your future.

To Youth on Race and Creeds

All human beings are brothers and sisters because in spite of all that divides them – race, language, nationality, religion – they are alike; each and every one of them is a human person.

☩

We call brothers and sisters those who are children of the same parents, of the same fathers and mothers. According to the teaching of Christ (and also according to the general religious view) people are brothers and sisters because God is their Father.

☩

Christ places this truth about the Fatherhood of God at the centre of his Gospel.

☩

He taught his disciples to pray, beginning with the words, 'Our Father' (Mt. 6:9)

☩

This prayer is a great help to us for loving our neighbour, and in particular for loving people who are hostile to us. It includes the words: 'Father . . . forgive us our trespasses as we forgive those who trespass against us' (Mt. 6:12)

To Buddhists and Shintoists: we express our esteem for your high spiritual values, such as purity, detachment of heart, love for the beauty of nature and benevolence and compassion for everything that lives. On this earth we are all pilgrims to the Absolute and Eternal, who alone can save and satisfy the heart. Let us seek his will together for the good of all humanity.

Violence is always an offence, an insult to man, both to the one who perpetrates it and to the one who suffers it.

✠

Violence is an offence against man but it is an offence above all against the Christian, because the Christian always recognises, in all men, brothers, and never enemies.

✠

I appeal to young people, do not listen to voices which speak the language of hatred, revenge, retaliation. Do not follow any leaders who train you in ways of inflicting death.

✠

It is necessary to say with forcefulness and conviction that a world of justice, solidarity and peace cannot be constructed on blood and on the corpses of victims, whose only crime is to have different views.

✠

Answer blind violence and inhuman hatred, beloved young people, with the impelling power of love! Bear witness with your behaviour, with your lives, that ideas are not imposed but are proposed.

✠

Only love, in fact, which is the soul of the Gospel, enables us to be always young. You know the outbursts of violence of our days; how many deaths they cause and how many tears! Well, he who causes death is not only old, but is already dead inside. Life, in fact, springs only from Love. So cultivate the most genuine love for everyone, like that of Jesus, always ready to help those in need, to forgive those who offend you, and even to correct or at least have compassion on those who act tyrannically.

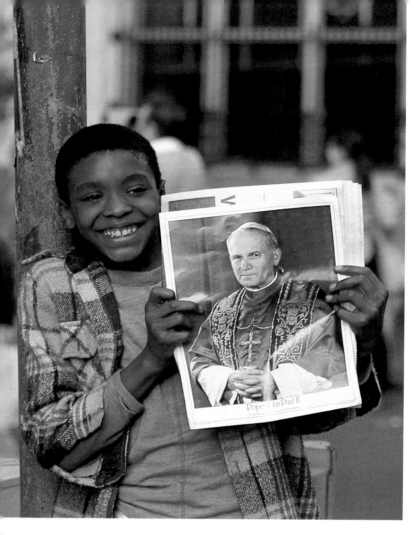

To Teenagers

I believe in Youth with all my heart.

⊹

Christ believes in you – everyone of you, And He loves you and wants to love through you! Amen.

⊹

Your task is crystal clear: to bring Christ to the world and to bring the world to Christ.

⊹

Only a constant turning to Him will give you fulfilment and joy.

⊹

A repeated conversion of heart becomes the condition for the usefulness of your activities and the attainment of your destiny.

Beloved young people, yours is always the noisiest presence but also the most likeable!

✠

The world of tomorrow is in your hands. Always look to Christ. He represents the most perfect model of every human existence.

✠

Your efforts of commitment and search are constantly accompanied by my prayer.

We must always prepare if we wish to do great things in life. Important things cannot be improvised.

✠

Young people, I say to you, Christ is waiting for you with open arms. Christ is relying on you to build Justice and Peace, to spread Love.

✠

May your faith be joyful, because it is based on awareness of possessing a Divine gift. When you pray and talk with God and when you converse with men, show the joy of this enviable possession.

If man trusts his own strength the world can offer him only prospects of death, drugs, violence, terrorism, tyranny, consumerism of every kind.

The opposite of all that is life, love, peace, joy, freedom, truth, respect for man.

In our age we are witnesses of a terrible exploitation of the words: love and freedom. The real meaning of these words must be found again. You must return to the Gospel. You must return to the school of Christ. Then you will transmit these spiritual goods; the sense of justice in all human relationships, the promotion and safeguarding of peace. The necessary support for these values lies only in the possession of a certain and sincere faith, a faith that embraces God and man, man in God. Where there is God and where there is Jesus Christ, his Son, this foundation is a solid one; it is deep, very deep. There is not a more suitable, a deeper dimension to be given to this word 'man', to this word 'love', to this word 'freedom', to these words 'peace' and 'justice'; there is no other but Christ.

In Christ is your search for those precious gifts that you young people must transmit to future generations, to the world of tomorrow; with him it will be easier and it cannot but succeed. I wish to raise you to this vision of transcendence and beauty, from which your Christian life will acquire solidity and go from strength to strength and bloom – because you are young and you must bloom. Let them be a promise of a more human and therefore more serene future. This age of ours is sad and will be sadder if it does not see that perspective which only you young people can give to it, to our generation, to our century, to our world!

Be convinced always that your daily work has great value in the eyes of God. Make every effort to ensure that its quality is worthy of Christ.

✠

Beloved young people, try to get to know Jesus in a true and comprehensive way. Deepen your knowledge of him in order to become friends with Him.

✠

It is knowledge of Jesus which ends loneliness, overcomes sadness and uncertainty, gives real meaning to life, curbs passions, exalts ideals, expands energies in charity, brings light in decisive choices. And only Jesus can give you real joy which is not superficial.

My very dear young people, I am happy to be with you. I greet you with a most heartfelt feeling, that of a Father and a Pastor.

☩

I thank you warmly for the consolation you afford me in seeing you so full of life, exuberance and joy.

☩

It is this display of joy of your spirit that catches my attention and inspires this brief exhortation of mine in our joyous meeting of hearts.

You are called to the discovery or rediscovery that is the Good News brought upon the earth by Jesus.

✠

Learn to unite your efforts in order to assure this joy to yourselves and whoever you encounter on the path of your day, in the family, school, work and play.

✠

There are youths like yourselves who have not yet found it.

✠

There are busy men and women who do not have the time and spirit to seek it.

✠

There are sick people in hospitals and old people in the homes who suffer from abandonment and loneliness.

✠

All these sisters and brothers await a smile from you, a word from you, your help, your friendship, and your handshake.

✠

Do not deny anyone the joy that comes from such gestures; thus you will bring comfort to them together with benefit to yourselves, because as Sacred Scripture says; 'It is more blessed to give than to receive.' (Acts 20:35)

Welcome, beloved in Christ! Your presence, so joyful and spontaneous, bears witness that the Church is young and projected towards the future. Be aware of your responsibilities; the message of Christ is entrusted to your generosity and your enthusiasm. You will have to take it into the new millennium, which is appearing on the horizon.

✠

It is an exacting message; it proclaims redemption by means of the cross, life and joy through suffering and death – it proclaims Christ crucified, who died and rose again. If you wish to be credible witnesses to it, make an effort above all to incarnate it in your lives. Those who approach you must be able to gather in your words, in your acts, in everything that you are, a reflection of the luminous face of the risen Christ.

✠

Jesus wishes to walk with you along the ways of the world, which is being constructed in these difficult years – do not forget it! I give you my Apostolic Blessing.

To Youth on Families

Dear young people, know that the Pope loves you, thinks of you and worries about you, would want you to be always good and happy and for this intention he offers his prayers.

✠

Remember you are part of a family. Love your family! Love your parents and all who love you!

✠

Love your families with generosity, patience, tact, tolerating those imperfections which are not lacking in any person whatsoever.

✠

Make your homes an oasis of peace and confidence.

✠

Pray with your families!

✠

Prepare yourselves also to form families of your own in the future. Do it in such a way that your love will always remain pure and serene through intimate friendship with Jesus.

✠

Offer your hearts and your youth to the Madonna of Grace for her help and protection.

✠

Dear young people, let my Blessing help you, which I impart to you with affection.

To children, who so often become a joyful presence on my way, I offer my special prayer, so that they may be brought up as good Christians in imitation of the most sublime model – Jesus, the God made man.

✠

To you, dear boys and girls, who are in the bloom of life, I express the cordial wish that you may go through the whole journey of life with the same fortune as the two wayfarers going to Emmaus. I exhort you to be witnesses to Easter joy and to the resurrection of Christ along the roads of the world, in your families, in your cities, in your environment of study and play. I bless you all willingly.

I hope that you all find in your homes an atmosphere of real love. Some-thing which has great value at your age is attachment to your family, especially your parents. I wish to invite you to establish and always main-tain a relationship of great and true affection with your parents; they are your first friends. To a large extent, your life in the future depends on how you are today in harmony with, and cherish respect for, those who begot you and brought you up.

✠

Certainly, the moment of detachment may come and for this, too, you must train for personally responsible growth; but never cut your family roots, for danger of becoming arid or wild.

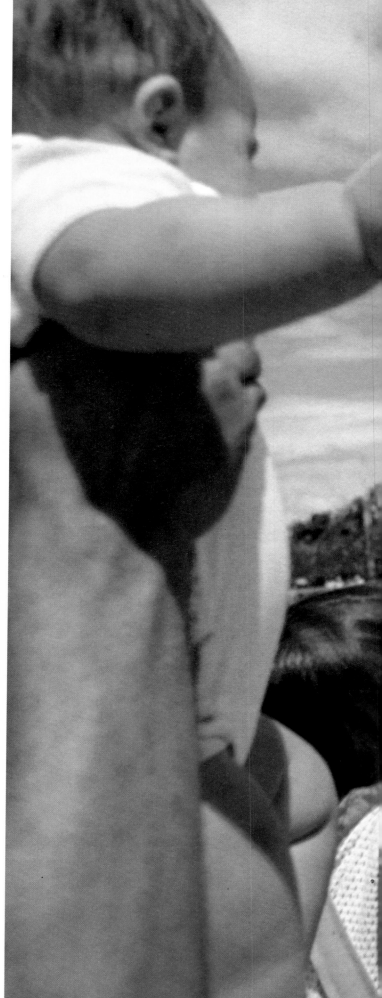

To Youth in Trouble

The young are for me a growing source of hope and joy, because when they are won over by Christ, they give everything, like the boy in the Gospel (Jn. 6:9) who offers his loaves and his fish, which gives rise to a miracle. To you my blessing, may it accompany you throughout your lives.

It would be lovely and consoling to meet you individually.

I want each of you to feel that this greeting of mine is addressed to you personally. It desires to be a moment of personal meeting, an instant of conversation and intimacy. The Pope feels particularly close to all those who are, in some way, in a situation of hardship and need.

I know your problems, I understand your difficulties; I know, in particular, how difficult it is for you to emerge from your intimate and unconfessed anguish and look to the future with confidence. However, I would like you to become aware of the strength, unforeseeable and concealed, that lies in your youth, which is such as to be able to blossom out in an industrious future. Sometimes we are lamps without light, with possibilities not realised. Well, I want to light in your hearts a flame, should the disappointments you have suffered, the expectations that have not come true, have extinguished it.

I want to say to each of you that you have capacities for good, honesty and industry; real, deep capacities, often unsuspected, sometimes made even greater by hard experience itself.

Rest assured that I love you and have confidence in you. I would like to show to you personally this affection, this trust of mine, and to tell you that I do not fail to raise my prayer to God so that He may always sustain you with that love which He showed by sending us His son, Jesus Christ, our Brother. He, too, experienced suffering and need, but he indicated to us the way and offers us His help to overcome them.

If you should sometimes be seized by the sad thought; 'people look at me with eyes that humiliate and mortify; perhaps even my dear ones do not have confidence in me'; well, rest assured that the Pope addresses you with esteem, as youths who have the capacity of doing so much good in life tomorrow and he relies on your responsible integration in society.

⁜

Let each of you consider within yourselves – your future cannot be constructed without your responsible co-operation. You are, in fact, the real architects and the ones mainly responsible – on the human level – for your future. May the light of Jesus make you understand the depth of the commitment that is required of you.

⁜

Life is a real gift from God, which is always worth accepting gratefully and courageously, in awareness that, from an existence lived with honesty, faithfulness and hope, you will be able to draw concrete satisfaction and ensure valuable advantages for society. This task may seem superior to your strength, but you are not alone in tackling it since the Lord, our Father and friend, has your personal destiny at heart in a far more effective and loving way than you can, perhaps, imagine. Present in us by the grace received at Baptism, He loves us faithfully even when we fail and He never leaves us alone in any circumstance. Therefore, turn with extreme confidence to Him who is beside you, in you, and be encouraged and strengthened by the affectionate Blessing which I impart to you.

I would like to bring to the young, with all the love of which I am capable, help for their growth, for their human formation, for the achievement of human responsibility which will make them capable of effecting free choices.

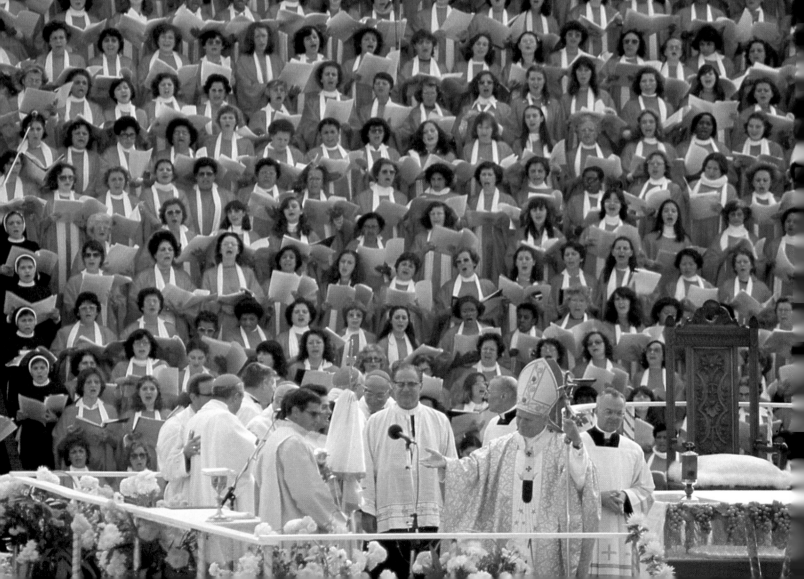

To Youth who Love Music

I have a deep feeling for the beauty of music and I am very fond of singing.

✠

I have a particularly deep feeling for liturgical music – Gregorian chant – but I also like contemporary music; Gershwin, for example, and Armstrong, Taki Rentaro and others. Naturally, I particularly enjoy Chopin and Szymanowski, but I also like Beethoven, Bach and Mozart.

Sacred Music is a synthesis of Art and Faith. Singing it is a manifestation of faith. In your behaviour there must be perfect harmony and real consistency between your singing and your life.

☩

Those who sing to God – St. Augustine tells us – live of God; those who psalmodize to His name, act for His glory.

☩

If you are true Christians, with your singing you will be evangelisers, that is messengers of Christ, in the modern world! Amen!

Communion and Liberation lives through an experience of song that creates Communion, I have known this experience for so many years — communion is lived through song.

✠

I have spent many hours (especially during my vacations) singing with young people.

✠

I am not surprised when it is said that in Heaven the Angels sing!

We walk in the light of God, in the joy of God. We are all involved in this pilgrimage. Let us go forward, let us walk and sing, as St. Augustine tells us: 'Not to satisfy tranquillity, but to comfort fatigue.' Let us do as travellers are wont to: sing, sing, but walk; console weariness with song, do not be content with idleness; sing and walk. Advance in good, advance in sound faith, advance in the good life.

✠

In this walking may we always be with Jesus, the Son of God and the Son of Mary; to Jesus, the Redeemer of man.

To Youth who are Sick or Disabled

The quality of a society and a civilization are measured by the respect shown to the weakest of its members.

You sick ones are very dear to me. God certainly looks on you with special affection because you resemble more his Son in the pain and humiliation of the Cross. I realise how hard your lives are, and how you may sometimes be overcome by dismay. But I exhort you with a fatherly heart, always to look up to where light and grace come from. And furthermore, the Church is purified every day by your sufferings united with those of the Lord. With these sentiments I am close to you always and I bless you.

To all the sick I say: rest assured the Pope is close to you in affection and daily prayer.

Be confident, the Lord will not abandon you. In the most difficult moments of trial turn to him and say with the same words I suggested in Brazil:—Lord, grant us patience, serenity and courage; grant us to live in joyful charity, for love of you, with those who are suffering more than ourselves and with those who, though not suffering, have not a clear view of the meaning of life.

Your suffering can be compared to the seed which, in the season of Winter, develops slowly, while awaiting to blossom in the Spring. Such is the suffering of a sick person; a precious seed which will receive unhoped for rewards from the Lord, a symbol of that Cross which regenerated the world and caused the buds of Christian communities to bloom everywhere. The Pope remembers you in prayer and blesses you willingly.

Dear, sick people, if you can raise your eyes to Heaven and take the inheritance of tears from God, you too will have a part in the song of heavenly life, which never passes away.

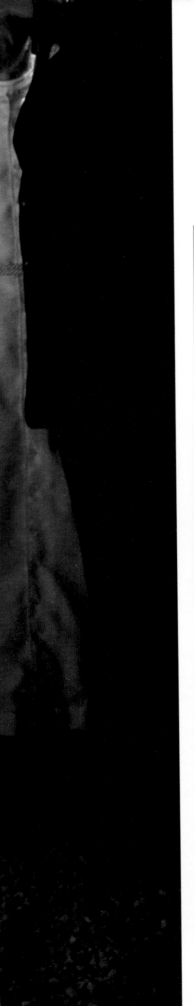

To the sick and disabled — a special word of confidence and encouragement. Of confidence, because the Church relies a great deal on the value of your suffering, which in the hands of the Lord may become very fruitful for the good of all. Of encouragement, because I assure you of my affection and my prayer so that you will be able to carry your cross joyfully with the help of God's grace, which I invoke, abundant and comforting for you all.

Beloved sick ones, the Pope esteems you highly and thanks you for the very important contribution that each of you makes with his own suffering to the life of the Church. Take heart: suffering passes but having suffered remains as a lasting claim to merit before God and men. May my Apostolic Blessing comfort you.

To all Blind people — I know well what noble sentiments distinguish you and with what dignity you bear your sufferings.

May your interior fortitude be a source of light and inspiration for those who have eyes to see, but often do not see, because they are unable to go beyond material appearances. The Church is grateful to you for the strength and example with which you are able to suffer and irradiate the eternal values of the spirit which put us into communion with God. As a sign of my special benevolence, I give you the Apostolic Blessing which I extend to all who accompany you and assist you.

To a group of lepers, (Marituba Colony in Belem)
I wish to remind you that in union with the mystery of Christ's Cross, the cross of your suffering too becomes a source of grace, life and salvation. I, for my part, also rely on you. Just as I ask for the help of the prayers of monks and sisters and so many holy persons, so that the Holy Spirit may inspire and give strength to my pontifical ministry, in the same way I ask for the valuable help that can come from the offering of your sufferings and your illness. Let this offering unite with your prayers, or better still let it be changed into prayer for me, for my direct collaborators, for all those who entrust to me their afflictions and their sorrows, their needs and their intentions.

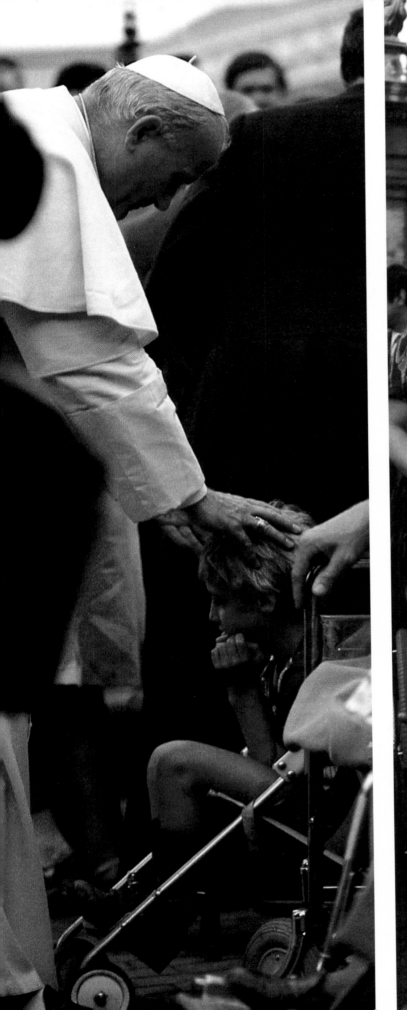
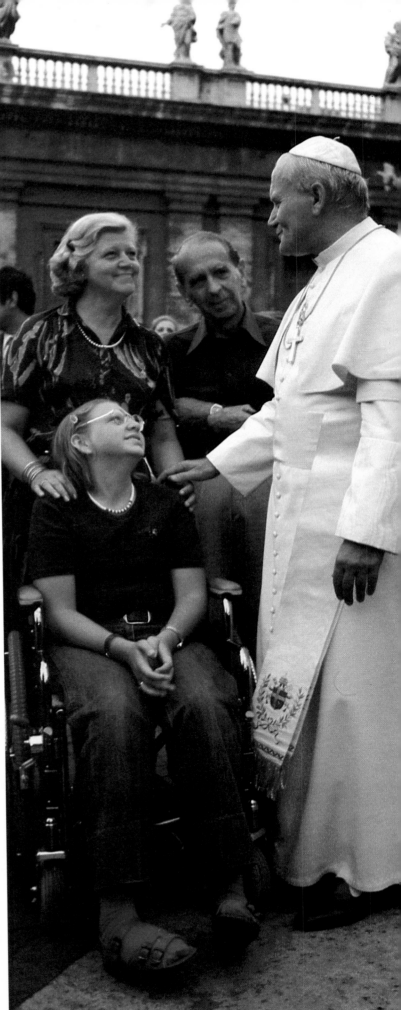

A special embrace for you, dear, sick disabled brothers! You represent through your very condition human weakness and at the same time the power and mercy of God. I am close to you with my affection and even more with prayer; but in my turn I commend the needs of the whole Church to your prayers, which are so powerful with God, who 'chose the weak in the world to shame the strong' (1 Cor. 1:27) May my comforting Apostolic Blessing help you for this.

✠

Dear friends, the Pope looks to you with sincere affection. He has a particular regard for you and reserves for you a special memory in his prayers, in order that you may always be serene in infirmity, fervent in spirit and pleasing to the Lord! I exhort you never to consider yourselves unlucky or useless. Though subject to the experience of suffering, which is often accompanied by loneliness, discouragement and inactivity, you must experience the fact that illness, when accepted and lived in a Christian way, elevates and ennobles you. In fact according to the Apostle — suffering produces endurance, endurance produces character and character produces hope and hope does not disappoint but contributes to an increase of love of God in our hearts. May these thoughts, which I accompany with my fatherly blessing always be the reason for hope and comfort for you.

For the world of pain, for the sick and all who are suffering, I reserve my special memory, which becomes a prayer for all. In the midst of suffering, preserve hope and courage, remembering that, united with Christ's cross, your interior solitude is transformed into graces of salvation for you and the whole Church.

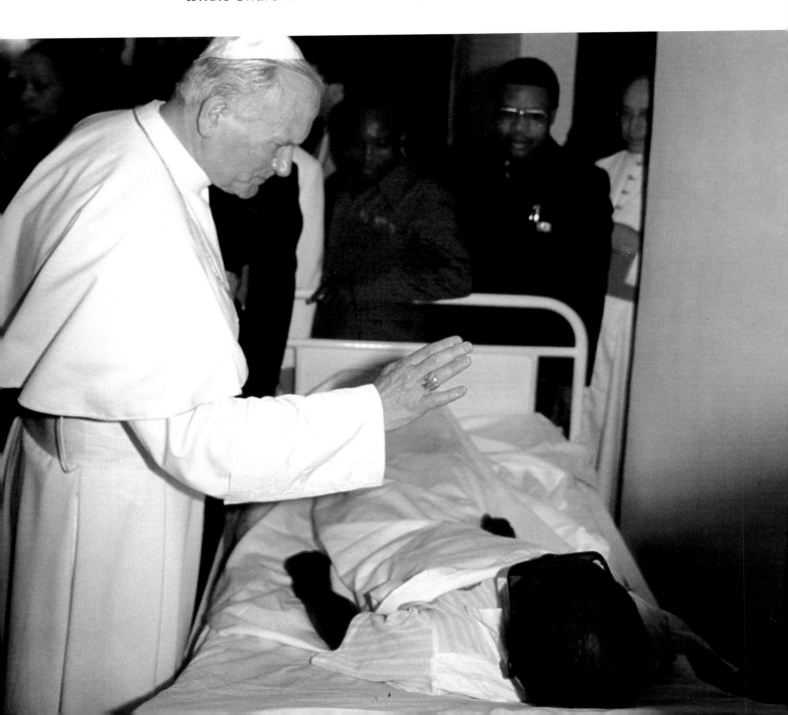

I am thinking of you, beloved sick. I wish to bring to you, tried in body and in the spirit, the immutable word of the Gospel: a word of consolation, confidence and solidarity and – if you allow me – of special affection. You know my concern for all the suffering, and this is an attitude which corresponds to the fundamental and primary duty of him who, succeeding Peter, has the formidable title of 'Vicar of Christ'.

☩

How could I represent Christ, if I forgot his constant concern for the sick, his exertions for them, the great words of faith addressed to them, his wonderful interventions, of which the pages of the Gospel are full? We read that the deaf and the blind, the crippled and the lame, paralytics and lepers flocked to Jesus from every part of Palestine, 'for power came forth from him and healed them all' (Lk. 6:19; cf. Mk. 1:32–34).

☩

How could I forget that 'mortal identification', which Jesus established between himself and the suffering, and inserts as a criterion of judgement – a demanding and severe judgement – in that code which will regulate our status for eternity?

☩

Christ lives and is hidden in your persons, as his own sufferings live again and continue in yours, so that that value, which we derive from Christ's blood, continues and increases by means of your own pain, according to what St. Paul tells us 'In my flesh I complete what is lacking in Christ's afflictions for the sake of his body, that is, the church' (Col 1:24; cf.2 Cor. 1:5; 12:9).

☩

Here, brothers and sisters, is the point of your being; your suffering is not sterile, it is not a plant that is wasted on the desert air, it is not blind and inexplicable cruelty. The Gospel in fact, explains it and interprets it: pain is direct participation in Christ's redeeming sacrifice and, as such, it has a precious function in the life of the Church. It is a mysterious but real treasure for all the faithful by virtue of that circulation of grace which Christ the head diffuses in his Mystical Body and which the members of this Body exchange with one another. I trust that these reminders will have the power to awaken in you, dear sick, renewed spiritual energies, which will also be beneficial – I firmly hope – for the desired recovery of your physical health.

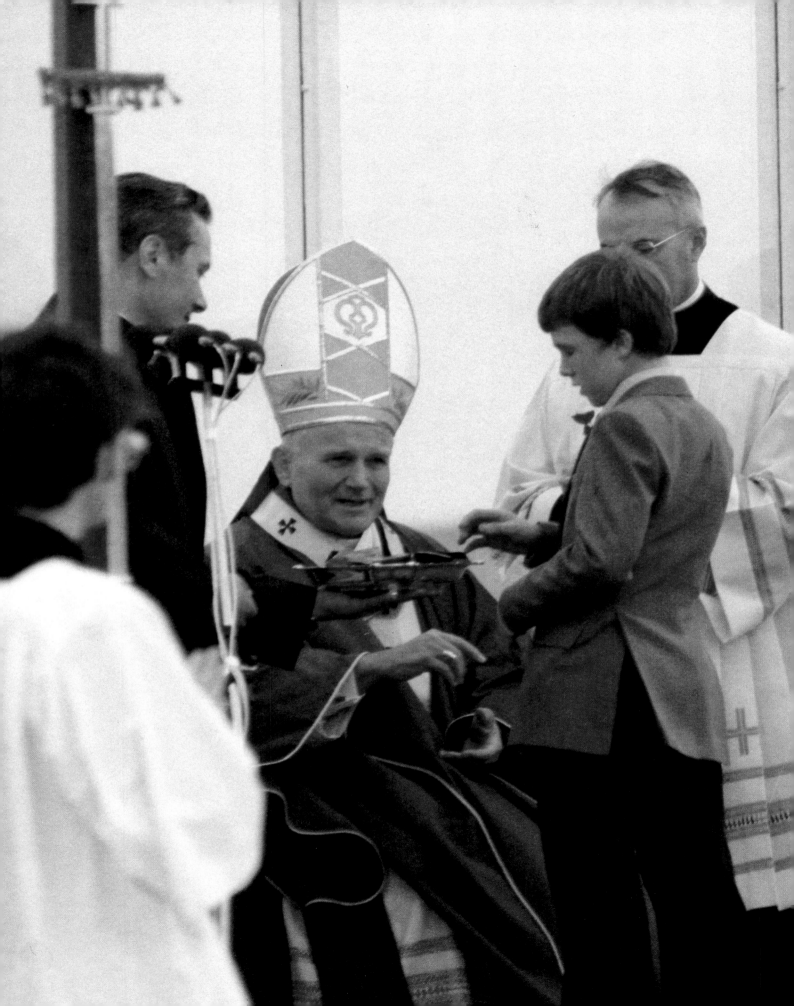

Questions and Answers
with Youth of Different Countries

In answer to a question from a youth in Paris – 'What do you speak of to rulers of the world when you meet them?'

Very often I speak to them precisely of the young. In fact the 'day of tomorrow' depends on youth. These words are taken from a song that young Poles often sing, 'It is on us that the day of tomorrow depends'. I, too, have sung it more than once with them.

Another question in Paris – 'We want to be happy. Is it possible to be so in the present-day world?' Pope John Paul quoted the Gospel Matthew 19. 16:22, then said –

Man can only be happy to the extent to which he is capable of accepting the requirements that his own humanity, his dignity as a man, set him, the requirements that God sets him. Christ's answer is absolutely original and cannot be outdated. You must think about it carefully and adapt it to yourselves.

✢

Christ's answer consists of two parts. In the first one, it is a question of observing the Commandments. Here I will digress on account of one of your questions on the principles the Church teaches in the field of sexual morality ('The Church always adopts decisions which are rather restrictive – why? Do you not fear youth will become estranged from the Church.'). *If you think deeply about this question, if you go to the heart of the problem, I assure you that you will realise one thing: in this field, the Church sets only the requirements that are closely linked with true, that is responsible, married and conjugal love. She demands what the dignity of the person and the fundamental social order requires. I do not deny they are her demands. But the essential point of the problem lies precisely there – namely that man fulfils himself only to the extent he is able to impose demands upon himself. Otherwise he goes away 'sorrowful' as we have just read in the Gospel. Moral permissiveness does not make man happy. The consumer society does not make man happy. They have never done so.*

In Paris and in the U.S.A., Pope John Paul was asked 'How does one pray as Pope?'

Like every Christian, he speaks – he listens. Sometime he prays without words and then he listens all the more. The most important thing is precisely what he 'hears'. and he also tries to unite prayer with his obligations, his activities, his work, and to unite his work with prayer. In this way, day after day, he tries to carry out his 'service', his 'ministry', which comes from the will of Christ and from the living tradition of the Church.

In Japan, the Pope was asked a number of different questions on Peace – one 18 year old student said 'We live in a society where it is possible to buy all we want – we are not at war with anyone – but in our peaceful society we are bored with all the money and time at our disposal – what can we do about this kind of peace?'
Part of the Pope's reply was:–

Since our time is limited, you will pardon me if in this series of questions – all of which are very important – I try to be concise in the responses, especially since I have the opportunity to speak on the theme of peace in other significant circumstances. One of my reasons for coming to Japan was in order to stop at Hiroshima; at the place where the first atomic bomb exploded, an event that represents a terrible warning. As I read the material which you sent, I noted that you are deeply concerned about the problem of peace – a true peace, as is right and natural, especially after the experience of 1945.

In your statements you note that peace cannot be based only on a balance of weaponry, that it cannot take the dominance of the strong over the weak as its presupposition, and that it cannot go hand in hand with any sort of imperialism. The Church thinks in the same way as you do and teaches in the same way. This was shown by the Second Vatican Council, by Pope John XXIII's Encyclical Pacem in Terris and by all the tireless activity of Pope Paul VI on behalf of peace, including the publication each year on the first of January of a special peace message. I am trying to continue this activity.

These are the themes of my peace messages: in 1979; 'To reach peace, teach peace'; in 1980; 'Truth, the power of peace'; in 1981; 'To serve peace, respect freedom'.

Peace must be built above all by those who are responsible for international decisions. However, they must bear in mind – as the Church keeps reminding us – that 'peace' means in the first place a true order in the relationship between individuals and nations. Thus, the building of peace from its foundations ought to mean recognising and so respecting all human rights, whether they concern the material aspect or the spiritual dimension of our earthly existence, and respecting the rights of all nations, without exception, whether large or small. Peace cannot exist if the great and powerful

violate the rights of the weak. I have spoken on this theme many times; I have done so at the United Nations Organization and at UNESCO. I wish to repeat it again in Japan.

⊹

If the programme of peace in the world is expressed in the saying 'Hiroshima never again', then it certainly is also expressed in the words 'Auschwitz never again'.

⊹

Thus, efforts to build peace in the world must be made at various levels. Peace does not mean standing still (as some of your opinions seem to express); it means an effort, and enormous effort, in which everyone has his own part to play. Awareness and a sense of responsibility must be stirred up. Solidarity must be shown with those whose rights are violated. We must 'see, judge, act'. Thus there is certainly much to be done, also by you young people. Here in Japan the future belongs to you. Think about the programmes for action in favour of peace – including those issued by the representatives of all the religions. The first of such conferences took place here in Japan in 1970, at Kyoto.

Christ says: 'Blessed are the peacemakers' (Mt. 5:9). Become peacemakers yourselves!

✠

The Christian religion, the religion that in a certain sense began with the words: 'Glory to God in the highest and on earth peace among men with whom he is pleased' (Lk. 2:14), first of all contributes to the cause of peace an ardent and incessant prayer which it invites us all to share in. It also contributes the conviction that man – including contemporary man – is capable, with the help of divine grace, of overcoming the many-sided evil that drives him along the paths of hatred, war and destruction. Man is capable of it. Christianity affirms this conviction and works for its strengthening. For it is animated by the words of Christ who is the teacher and witness of hope!

To the Youth of Frascati the Pope said:—

As I said to twenty thousand young people in Madison Square Gardens, New York,

✠

When you are astonished at your own mystery,
look to Christ who offers you the meaning of life.
When you seek to know what being a mature person means,
look to Christ who is the fullness of the human being.
And when you try to imagine what will be your role in
the future of the world — look to Christ.
It is only in Christ that you will fully reach your potential
both as men and women and as citizens.

I wish to express to you my exhortation to feel personally responsible for those of your own age who have not yet known the joy which comes from the discovery of friendship with Christ. Here are the instructions I leave with you, O beloved young people: bring Christ to your friends, bring your friends to Christ! You could not give them a greater gift.
To you all my Blessing, may it accompany you throughout your lives.

All extracts taken from the following issues of *Osservatore Romano*:

29. 8.79	28. 1.80	14. 4.80	16. 6.80	11. 8.80	13.10.80	9. 3.8
19.11.79	4. 2.80	28. 4.80	23. 6.80	8. 9.80	20.10.80	23. 3.8
24.12.79	18. 2.80	19. 5.80	30. 6.80	15. 9.80	3.11.80	6. 4.8
14. 1.80	17. 3.80	5. 5.80	14. 7.80	22. 9.80	12. 1.81	13. 4.8
21. 1.80	31. 3.80	2. 6.80	28. 7.80	29. 9.80	9. 2.81	5. 5.8

British Library Cataloguing in Publication Data

John Paul II, *Pope*
    Beloved young people.
    1. Youth—Religious life   2. Christian life
    1. Title
    248.8'3   BV4531.2
    ISBN 0-340-27966-4

Published by Hodder & Stoughton Children's Books,
a division of Hodder & Stoughton Ltd, Mill Road,
Dunton Green, Sevenoaks, Kent TN13 2YJ.

Printed in Italy by New Interlitho, Milan.
Origination by Adroit Photo Litho Limited, England.

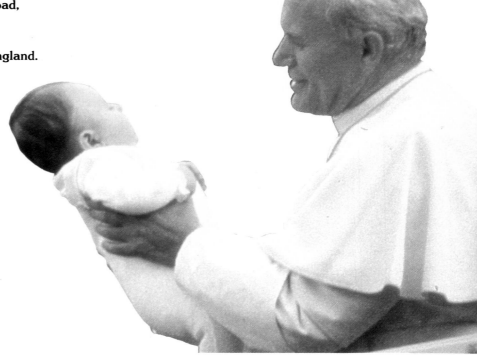